Leadership Essentials

Wisdom to Live by, Lead by and Grow by

Nolan W. McCants

Leadership Essentials
Copyright © 2007
By Nolan W. McCants

ISBN 978-0-9795711-0-7

Published by
McCants Ministries
P.O. Box 9352
Naperville, IL 60567-9352
630.904.6262

www.nolanmccants.com

All scripture quotations, unless otherwise indicated, are taken from the New King James Version. Copyright © 1982 by Thomas Nelson, Inc. Used by permission. All rights reserved.

Printed in the United States.

CONTENTS

DEDICATION

To the three distinguished leaders in my life who have helped to shape who I am today as a Christian leader:

- The late, Dr. James B. Alford who recognized the ministry calling on my life as a teenager, called it out, and then provided me with an incredible model of integrity to follow.
- Bishop Willie. J. Chambliss, who gave me the opportunity to develop my gift, and provided a safe place for me to fully surrender my all to God while walking into my destiny.
- Bishop Kirby Clements, who first inspired me to write, has never hesitated to offer a loving spanking and continues to speak solid wisdom into my life.

ACKNOWLEDGEMENTS

I thank God for the gift and the passion to write. Every good and perfect gift comes from Him (James 1:17), and He deserves all the glory for the words in this book.

Ministry done the right way is never a solo act. My love, appreciation, and gratitude goes out to my wife, Gloria, and our girls Staci and Joy, for providing the sanctuary of family.

To the crew: Monica Chambers, Michelle Frost, Joyel Hall and Gloria, for keeping the day-to-day ministry humming at Harvest. You guys enable me to express all of my gifts without guilt or fear of loss.

The Harvest Church Leadership Team, you're second to none.

My growing Harvest Church Plainfield family, thank you for allowing me to serve you all of these years. Keep your eyes fixed on God, continue to practice Matthew 6:33, and see what happens.

Simon Presland for your eyes, editing skills, and motivation.

All of the great leaders who graciously allow me to touch their lives and ministries, while they do great things for the kingdom of God and its awesome King.

FOREWORD

After twenty-five years of being a pastor, I am well aware of the importance of church growth and development. Helping a church grow from two hundred members to well over three thousand is no small feat; but with God's grace upon me, I've seen this happen in my own ministry. During this time, I've noticed that one of the most important but overlooked aspects of church growth is the selection of capable and qualified leadership who love the Lord.

In the past sixteen years I have repeatedly called upon Pastor Nolan McCants to offer his wisdom, insights, and strategies on the topic of leadership to my church family. I have seen him develop these in his own ministry at Harvest Church Plainfield—and they work! All praise be to God. His dedication, devotion, and discipline in the areas of church leadership and ministry development are unparalleled. He has been truly anointed in these areas, and his desire to share his experiences with the Body of Christ is a blessing to all. His giftings are much needed in the Church, especially given the tumultuous times in which we live.

After a recent illness, I understood anew the importance of having competent, compassionate, and capable leaders in place in every area of church life. Being out of the pulpit for over four months gave me a fresh perspective of my church that I could not see while in ministry. Nolan helped develop competent leadership at my church to fill the void created by my absence. His input assisted in furthering a strong and vibrant vision for my ministry that continues to expand today.

This book is one that I personally believe will help strengthen the leadership in churches everywhere. The apostle Paul said to Timothy: *"Study to show thyself approved unto God, a workman that needeth not to be ashamed, rightly dividing the word of truth"* (II Timothy 2:15). Although this scripture is in reference to understanding the Word of God, I also know that if you take hold of the words that Nolan offers, you will never be ashamed of your leadership abilities or of those in leadership around you. Just put what you learn into practice and see what God will do through you.

The leadership lessons in this book were developed from Nolan's daily devotions and church experiences. It is my prayer that you will be blessed by them, as I know you will. Your life or ministry will never be the same if you prayerfully take hold of the powerful principles that are set forth on the following pages. You will see God work

Foreword

through you and your ministry. Hallelujah! Blessed reading, and may our immeasurable God do for you and your ministry more than you could ask or imagine, according to his power that is at work within you (Ephesians 3:20). The tools to develop biblical leadership are now in your hands.

Pastor Marvin E. Wiley
Rock of Ages Baptist Church
Maywood, Illinois

INTRODUCTION

"Two are better than one, Because they have a good reward for their labor. For if they fall, one will lift up his companion. But woe to him who is alone when he falls, For he has no one to help him up" (Ecclesiastes 4:9-10).

In every family there are "elephants hiding under the carpet." These are subjects that need to be discussed, but nobody wants to tackle them. Some are small things, *(Mom doesn't look good in that dress)*, while others are essential *(dad has a real problem with his anger)*. In most cases, if these discussions took place, the affected relationships would improve and real growth experienced. Nevertheless, approaching delicate subjects will always require wisdom, timing, and the right motivation.

So it is in the family of God. When it comes to leadership, there are some things that we need to talk about, but are afraid to *(pride, greed and lust being the top three)*. There is no doubt that frank discussions about particular issues will lead to stronger relationships and a healthier church. With humility and a desire to help you experience success in your ministry and your walk with God, I offer you *Leadership Essentials.*

Whether in the business or church world, I've always had a heart for those in leadership. As an entrepreneur for over fifteen years, I was involved in the public relations industry where I was called upon by heads of companies throughout America. As a businessman, I learned the importance of building relationships with like-minded people, how to effectively network within my community, and how to be a strong leader with a servant's heart, amongst other leadership principles. When I became a pastor, God graciously taught me how to incorporate what I had learned into the church world. My experiences have allowed me to reach out to many leaders within the global church community, and I am grateful to God for these opportunities.

As the founder and senior leader of a growing church, *Harvest Church Plainfield,* I have been extremely fortunate to continue building meaningful relationships. I am privileged to enjoy healthy peer relationships where candor, vulnerability and integrity are esteemed. These relationships are priceless, as we have shared a mutual interest in continuing to grow as leaders, while building healthy ministries that make a difference.

I wrote this book from the perspective of having an open discussion with some of my friends that you too can benefit from. *Leadership Essentials* is the first in a series of

Introduction

books I will write. Written in an easy-to-read, plain language style, each chapter addresses a stand-alone topic that would benefit anyone serving in a ministry capacity. The pages are filled with practical wisdom and powerful insights that can be used to build solid ministry. I pray your life and ministry will be enriched by what is offered here.

Nolan W. McCants

CHAPTER 1

PRACTICING REST

Following His extraordinary feat of creating the heavens and the earth, God rested. Wow, what a concept! It may not have been the type of rest we require, but He certainly sent a message to mankind: Rest is an essential part of our lives. It is also a powerful expression of faith and something that should be practiced regularly. Rest is evidence that we believe the job is complete, so we rest from the work. Many people consider vacationing, getaways or leisure time a luxury. However, these are essential in maintaining our physical, emotional and spiritual health, and should have the same priority as your devotional time or your serving others.

It is important that we rest our mind and body each day from the rigors we face. As simple as this might seem, it is a common sense lesson that many in leadership have yet to learn. There will always be one more phone call or decision to make, or one more crisis to deal with. If taking time to rest isn't a part of your daily routine, then emotional and physical exhaustion are sure to come. In His wisdom, God instituted the Sabbath knowing we would get too consumed in life's affairs to slow it down and take a break. Here is what Jesus said to the disciples upon their return from a very powerful and productive ministry trip. *"And the apostles gathered themselves together unto Jesus, and told him all things, both what they had done, and what they had taught. And he said unto them, Come ye yourselves apart into a desert place, and rest a while: for there were many coming and going, and they had no leisure so much as to eat"* (Mark 6:30-31 KJV).

Sadly, I know many people in ministry who think rest is the first cousin to slothfulness; their excuses for not taking a vacation are some of the most creative I've ever heard. Of course *doing the work of the ministry* is always their justification. This begs the questions: Are we in ministry for ourselves or because Jesus called us? And if He called us, then shouldn't

WE OFTEN OVERLOOK THE PRACTICAL SIDE OF JESUS' LIFESTYLE AND MINISTRY, AND FOCUS ON THE MIRACLES.

we follow His example in taking time to rest? In the above verse, I'm sure that Jesus was just as excited as the disciples were in their experiencing God's life transforming power flowing through them. But he also wanted to teach them an invaluable lesson that would increase their potential to experience successful ministry for many years to come. We often overlook the practical side of Jesus' lifestyle and ministry, and focus on the miracles. I would imagine some of the *super spiritual disciples* were offended that Jesus would seemingly downplay their jubilant victory reports and emphasize their need to rest.

Rest is Not an Option

When rested you can love better, build better, serve better, think better, pray better, lead better, and overall you will just be better.

In Mark 6:31, Jesus' disciples had not stopped to rest long enough to eat a decent meal. He was concerned and wanted to make it clear to them that resting was not an option. This same lesson applies to us as well: regular intervals of rest are a necessity. While in business, I disciplined myself to take regular times of rest. Now that I'm in ministry I am even more resolute in doing so, and I won't apologize or carry guilt.

When I was younger, I learned to listen to my body. I could sense when I was over the top and could pull back. Over the years its become increasingly difficult to pick up these same warnings. When I am tired, my one clear indicator is that I become short with people, and I hate

WHEN RESTED YOU CAN LOVE BETTER, BUILD BETTER, SERVE BETTER, THINK BETTER, PRAY BETTER, LEAD BETTER, AND OVERALL YOU WILL JUST BE BETTER.

getting to that place. Often I can hide my frustrations and exhibit patience in the most difficult situations. But if I'm overtired and don't take time to rest, the bear in me comes out all too quickly. My wife, Gloria, will then say, "It's time isn't it?"

I'm sure the demands of ministry can drive you to overload quickly as well. You've got to know yourself and take time to rest when you feel the need coming on.

When we're overworked and void of sufficient rest, our perspective becomes distorted. Decisions are hastily made without clear thought, and our creative abilities ebb away. Wisdom says that taking time to rest keeps us fresh and focused.

Developing a Plan

When I was a young minister in training, my pastor, the late Dr. James B. Alford, would often wisely say, "Burning the candle at both ends may give you more light, but it will also burn faster too." He practiced what he preached by taking regular vacations as a demonstration of his proclamation. On his days off you could find him at home relaxing in his easy chair. To this day his words and life minister to me whenever I'm overextended.

Since I can no longer trust myself to know when to stop, I've factored into my annual planning quarterly getaways and alone time. Over the years, Gloria and I have enjoyed both planned and spontaneous escapes, some local and some long distance. For instance, as a young man working hard to build a business, I took frequent trips to Lake Geneva, a beautiful area of southern Wisconsin, a place I am still fond of. This continues to be one of my preferred getaway destinations. The quiet beauty and small town atmosphere provides the perfect setting for my personal rejuvenation. The duration of my trips there have varied over the years depending upon available time, money, and needed rest. Sometimes I go alone, occasionally with the entire family, and often with Gloria.

Gloria and I have also planned breaks together, with other couples, with the kids, as well as by ourselves. If you're married, I believe getaways with your mate should take precedence over all others. Before traveling with the entire family, I try to find alone time and unwind so that others don't experience the all-too-common burnout backlash. It's proven to be an excellent strategy. The kids can laugh all night and ask if we're there yet over and over, and Mr. Grumpy never comes out thanks to the pre-trip rest. There's nothing worse than taking a vacation and being so stressed that you trudge through each day attempting to wear a happy face over your misery, while trying to give what you really don't have.

For married couples, I think it's also a good idea to take separate trips as long as both spouses agree. This will bring renewal, and can restore vitality to your marriage. Separate breaks might not be a need for both of you. However, if one partner needs time alone, then the other should consider encouraging them and aiding in the planning process. The last time I checked, the marriage vows did not include a mandate to be joined at the hip. Of course this always works best when there is agreement.

It also pays to be spontaneous. One year I was on the phone with a client and friend who informed me about *another* exotic trip he was taking, this one to Acapulco, Mexico. He then mentioned the deal he had found and asked if Gloria and I would like to go along. It was February in Chicago and about ten degrees, need I say more? Days later we were strolling along the beaches of Acapulco under sunny skies and daily temperatures in the eighties. It was both romantic and refreshing. I should add that we managed not to discuss any business, as was agreed to before hand. No matter the frequency, whether alone or with family or friends, there has to be a plan. It won't just happen—that's why it's called *taking* a vacation.

The Guilt Factor

"Now it came to pass, as they went, that he entered into a certain village: and a certain woman named Martha received him into her house. And she had a sister called Mary, which also sat at Jesus' feet, and heard his word. But Martha was cumbered about much serving, and came to him, and said, Lord, dost thou not care that my sister hath left me to serve alone? bid her therefore that she help me. And Jesus answered and said unto her, Martha, Martha, thou art careful and troubled about many things: But one thing is needful: and Mary hath chosen that good part, which shall not be taken away from her" (Luke 10:38-42 KJV).

Do you know anyone like Martha who is guilt ridden whenever she takes a break and badgers others who know how to choose *the good part?* They're everywhere—at church, work, school, and home. Mary made a wise decision to pull back and rest at the feet of Jesus. Don't allow others to lay guilt trips on you, and refuse to succumb to self-imposed ones as well.

Many people suffer from guilt, fear, or the thought that if they aren't present somehow the "boat will cease

> **DON'T ALLOW OTHERS TO LAY GUILT TRIPS ON YOU, AND REFUSE TO SUCCUMB TO SELF-IMPOSED ONES AS WELL.**

to float." Others view vacations as a reward for working themselves crazy. But a vacation is more than a reward: it is a necessity. I once overheard a conversation between two top-level executives. The younger one had recently been promoted to an unprecedented level within the company and was eager to prove his worth. On this particular day he was not feeling well, and had not been for days. The wiser, older, executive shared a simple parable with him. "Do you remember when Mr. Jones passed away? Did any of the Jones stores close?" he asked. "No," the younger man replied. "So what do you think would happen if you died today?" The message instantly became clear. "Go home and get some rest," the wise executive said. "Your job and all of its worries will be here tomorrow when you return."

Don't be afraid to relax; it's not a sin. I checked. Nor are we expected to work until we literally fall at the feet of Jesus. Unfortunately for some this manner of doing ministry is considered commendable. They believe they will receive an extra reward for working overtime in the *works* department. The truth is there will be no rewards for foolishly overextending ourselves. I believe that Jesus knew His disciples—like most of us—would use ministry as an excuse to work perpetually. I feel this is why He quickly turned their attention from their successful mission, and onto their need for rest. In today's world, many in ministry are adrenaline junkies and overachievers who like surfing the waves of momentum, and find it difficult to rest. Some have attained a measure of success, yet are driven by the fear of losing what they have gained; they want to hold to what they believe they have achieved. My advice is simple: let it go, and you'll find out that rest is just as important as the work you do.

Beware! Guilt can surface from various places:
- Demands of society, the rat race
- The workplace culture
- Over-zealous church workers and leaders
- An overachieving attitude
- The thought of being undeserving
- A works mentality
- Self-imposed guilt

Travel Destinations

I like traveling to a variety of resting places. One of my favorite spots to visit is the Mill Valley area of California, just north of San Francisco. The combination of the ocean,

Practicing Rest

mountains, palm trees, and their microclimates provide both therapy and creative stimulation. I've often gone there to relieve my stress and anxiety. I've return rejuvenated with renewed passion, clarity of vision, and the patience to take on the best metal testers.

When it comes to ministry, the drain on your mental and emotional state varies. Depending on the volume of work and the type of activity, you may need different forms of rest. For me, there are times when I crave the solitude of Wisconsin, and other times when I need to have my creative juices stirred and stimulated. This may call for a trip to Las Vegas or Disney World. These two destinations are places where creativity is constantly being redefined. Technology and resources from around the world are employed to captivate their target markets, and I'm re-energized every time I visit. The key is to know yourself and choose your place of rest based on your present emotional, physical, and spiritual state.

Mini-Vacations

Travel distance is an important factor when choosing where to take a mini-vacation. For frequent but short breaks—perhaps once a quarter—it is best if the location is within a two-hour drive. In my case, the sooner I can reach my destination, the better I feel. Conversely, some people find that driving is just as relaxing as staying in one place. Whatever works for you is the best plan to follow, but be sure to take the necessary time.

~25~

Micro-Breaks

While stress is a fact of life, getting away for extended periods of time isn't always feasible. Now, for you excuse makers, I don't want you to add this to your list. The truth is that sometimes you need a quick escape from all the madness, but leaving home isn't possible. This calls for some creativity. There are many simple ways that I call micro-breaks. For instance, a few years ago I was in Atlanta visiting with mentors and dear friends, Bishop Kirby and Sandra Clements. They have a way of relaxing the formalities and weaving a visit into their everyday lives. While there I witnessed one of their relaxation routines. After a peaceful dinner at a Thai restaurant, we strolled through the mall, enjoying a leisure evening of window shopping. It was their way of unwinding. I guess as long as there are no credit cards available, I'd be willing to try this with my wife too!

My point is that finding the time and appropriate place to rest doesn't have to be involved, expensive or difficult. For example, I am blessed to live less than an hour outside of Chicago. A world-class city, it has many diversions to offer. A visit to the lakefront alone can take you away better than a Calgon bath. Walks down north Michigan Avenue, or a visit to the Museum Campus are a couple ways my family and I experience rest.

I found another way right in my own backyard. A few years ago, I was driving through my neighborhood and realized I knew every street, pass through, and hideaway in the neighborhood I grew up in. However, driving to and from work had alienated me from my present home environment. After some thought, I decided to take up walking. Gloria and I began walking three to five miles a day, at least three times a week. Strolling along the trails and across the bridge-covered ponds in our subdivision has also provided us with quality time to exercise and talk.

I also like to fish, but unlike some of my friends and family, I don't consider fishing to be serious business. I like putting the worm on the hook, dropping the line in the water, and relaxing. If I actually catch something, that's a bonus. To me the whole point is to spend time outdoors soaking up the sunshine, and feeling the warmth while I rest my mind.

Recently Gloria and I decided to establish a daily quiet time in our home. For an hour and a half each weekday we turn off the television and only take selective phone calls; it's amazing what an intrusion these are. Some days we're in the family room together with our girls, working on homework and projects. Other times we're reading a book or working at the computer.

Whatever relaxes you and allows you to get away from routine hustle and bustle, I encourage you to take deliberate and regular times of rest.

Friends and Family

Combining rest with visiting family or friends might seem like a good idea. You may even feel you're being efficient, but often these visits only serve to increase your stress levels. Your host might have a hidden agenda that will demand your time, but won't be revealed until the middle of breakfast. Save yourself. During your times of rest, give yourself license to be selfish. That's right, be *selfish*. Serve yourself first. Once you've rested, then visit with friends or relatives wearing a genuine smile and fortified with the patience of Job.

Ministers are also notorious for attending conferences and calling it a vacation break. It's true that some conferences build in leisure time, but this isn't the type of rest I'm talking about. You need time away from your cell phone, networking, and the business of ministry. Give yourself permission to get away from all of these distractions and unwind.

Establishing Rules

It's important to establish rest rules for yourself and with those around you. When our children were younger, Gloria and I would enjoy regular date nights. My mother,

DO NOT HESITATE TO ASK THOSE AROUND YOU TO HONOR YOUR WISH FOR PEACE AND QUIET.

who passed away in 2004, would keep them and guard the telephone. If our girls attempted to call she would explain that mom and dad needed time to be alone. She helped protect us from burnout, a measure of loving support that we've missed very much.

While I'm away, my office staff directs all matters to appropriately trained and assigned personnel. I leave with the knowledge that some things may even fall apart. What's my attitude? If it's not essential or life threatening, either the team can handle it or I will upon my return. Do not hesitate to ask those around you to honor your wish for peace and quiet and to assist you in meeting this objective. Arrange your ministry so that it can run without you for brief periods. Trust me, whatever and whomever you left will still be there when you return.

Making it Happen

Vacations, getaways and excursions can be costly. If you have the financial means, do it. If finances are a challenge you'll need to become resourceful. When Gloria and I started the church we struggled financially, and it was difficult to maintain our home, not to mention taking a vacation. We decided to take micro-breaks, then moved up to mini-vacations when finances allowed.

Following the first-year anniversary of our ministry, we had about one hundred fifty dollars and a real need for a break. We took our girls, then ages three and four, to Lake Geneva, Wisconsin, a little over an hours drive from our home. We didn't have any reservations, just a need and the belief that God would provide. We pulled into a small Christian-owned motel, and I shared my story with the front desk attendant. I explained that we had limited funds, were celebrating our freshman year in the pastorate, and needed two nights stay at their facility. I offered to pay seventy-five dollars for the two nights. He said that was fine as long as we made our own beds and used the same towels. We agreed and enjoyed a mini-vacation on a shoestring. Thank God that our girls were so young; at that age they had no idea we weren't at a Marriott.

As the congregation grew, a number of businessmen and women joined us. Many of them traveled, and I thought that someone might have excess frequent flyer miles they could part with. Sure enough a couple of guys freely surrendered theirs. You could check within your sphere of ministry, because the last thing a frequent traveler wants to see is another airport, and you could be the beneficiary.

One Kansas City church gives their pastor and his wife gift certificates for a two-week stay at a major hotel chain. They can use these anytime, a couple days at a time or the entire two weeks at once. Another way to reduce your expenses is through the use of credit cards that offer points towards free flights and hotel stays. I am not suggesting that you go into debt to pay for a vacation. Rather, I encourage you to pay your bills using your credit card and then pay off the card with the same money you would have used to pay your bills. Your points will add up fast and can be earned on both personal and business cards.

Another option is to join the various free travel programs offered by hotels, airlines, and rental car agencies. Be sure to read the fine print though, because all programs are not created equally. Some offer better deals, allowing you to earn freebies faster, while others may charge hidden fees for transferring or accessing points. When you combine the use of points earned on credit cards with those from frequent traveler programs you can double your point accumulation. I've had many people ask me if I'm independently wealthy because of my travel. I love removing the mystery by explaining my strategy for vacationing on a budget.

If you like a particular destination, get to know the people at the hotels, particularly the small boutique hotels. Remember names of people who gave you excellent service. Write thank you notes and letters to their bosses. They will not forget your efforts and they will pay off on future visits with upgrades and other perks.

Finally, before calling to book a room, check rates on the hotel's Internet site; most offer slightly better deals on-line. If you call a hotel's front desk, let them know you saw a particular rate on-line and that you want it. If they refuse, book it on-line. A week or two before you travel, check the rates on-line again. If the hotel has booked fewer guests than anticipated, their rates may have dropped. Call the hotel, give your confirmation number, tell them you saw a lower rate on-line, and request an adjustment. During my travels, I've had my rate reduced many times using this strategy.

Now, forget the thought that travel is too costly, and start making plans to get some well-deserved rest and relaxation.

Commit to Doing This for You

- *Leave ALL work behind*
  Unless it is a working trip, leave your to-do list at home. Resist the temptation to bring along things that can rob you of true rest.

- *Turn the cell phone off and say no to email*
  This may be difficult to imagine, but for years we all functioned wonderfully without these modern conveniences. Record a message stating you will return calls upon the date of your return. Invite them to call your office or designated person in the meantime. Give office staff specific guidelines for contacting you while you're away. The same can be done with email.

- *Learn your signs of fatigue*
  We all overreact when we're fatigued. We have to learn our own warning signs and respond appropriately.

- *Become disciplined in your rest time*
  Get rid of the excuses. Make rest a planned priority.

- *Don't be afraid to be selfish*
  Here is one time that selfishness is permissible. Take care of yourself so that you can better take care of others.

- *Encourage those you serve with to rest as well*
  Since we reproduce ourselves, I'm sure that an *all work and no play* mentality has been woven into your culture. Encourage those around you to take time to rest. You may even need to share your frequent travelers points at times to make it possible.

CHAPTER 2

GRACE TO SERVE

*"Now therefore, behold, the cry of the children of Israel has come to
Me, and I have also seen the oppression with which the Egyptians oppress
them. Come now, therefore, and I will send you to Pharaoh that you may
bring My people, the children of Israel, out of Egypt." But Moses said to God,
"Who am I that I should go to Pharaoh, and that I should bring the children
of Israel out of Egypt?"*

*Then Moses said to the LORD, "O my Lord, I am not eloquent, neither
before nor since You have spoken to Your servant; but I am slow of speech
and slow of tongue." So the LORD said to him, "Who has made man's mouth?
Or who makes the mute, the deaf, the seeing, or the blind? Have not I, the
LORD? Now therefore, go, and I will be with your mouth and teach you what
you shall say"* (Exodus 3:9-11, 4:10-12).

Like Moses, there are only a few people who have
answered the call of God on their lives and felt sufficient for
the job at hand. The thought of ministry can be exhilarating.
However, facing the daily realities of ministry is often
overwhelming. Representing the Creator of the heavens
and the earth can be awe-inspiring, as Moses quickly found
out. Whether serving as pastor, secretary, mom, dad, Sunday

School teacher, or an usher, there is always an unrelenting sense of inadequacy.

There are a couple things that Moses did wrong that we are guilty of as well. First, he looked down before he looked up. His immediate response to God's call was to consider

IT'S VERY IMPORTANT TO BECOME COMFORTABLE WITH WHO WE ARE, BECAUSE GOD IS.

his own frailties rather than look to God's power and might. Performance was also an issue with Moses. He wondered how he could possibly do what God had called him to do, considering that he was less than a dynamic orator, or even may have suffered with a speech impediment that rocked his confidence. He may have seen some great performers in his day and began to cave in under the *pressure to perform*. This is not uncommon. How often do we hesitate to move forward because we've compared ourselves to others?

It's very important to become comfortable with who we are, because God is. When God gave you your assignment, He knew all about your strengths and weakness, none of which came as a surprise to Him. Know that you are distinctively you and that's a good thing. God doesn't want you to be anybody else. He can express Himself through you like nobody else on earth. I was liberated from the "comparison syndrome" some years ago when a friend told me that most people compare their weak side to another's strong side. This viewpoint always leads to our minimizing ourselves, or worse, ignoring our own strengths. From that point forward, I began to see just how uniquely God had designed me and began to value myself. I soon became comfortable with myself. Sure, there are people who can do some things a lot better than me, but I am fully in touch with my gifts and strengths.

Second, it is important to remember that we have not called ourselves to do God's bidding; He called us. We are not personally responsible for the outcome of the ministry He has given us. The Scriptures say, some plant, others water, but it is God alone who can give increase (see I Corinthians 3:7). There is no need to compete or compare yourself with others when you're doing what God has called you to do. Faith and obedience are the currency of the kingdom. When you do what God has directed you to do and you trust Him to provide, you experience great success in all that you have been commissioned to do. We are indeed limited in our ability to affect ministry or life without Him. Our role is to follow His lead and look to Him for all that we need, including the ability to finish the assigned task, *"for it is God who works in you both to will and to do for His good pleasure"* (Philippians 2:13).

Facing Feelings of Inadequacy

When operating in the world without Christ, we use things, position, power, and walls of pride to conceal our feelings of inadequacy. But when we serve God, we are free to become naked and fully exposed before Him.

Feelings of inadequacy are a part of ministry life. In fact, they are part of life itself. Paul talked of the thorn in his flesh,

FEELINGS OF INADEQUACY ARE A PART OF MINISTRY LIFE.

Jacob wrestled with God, the Psalmist was curious as to why God had such interest in man. There is that persistent conflict within us that stirs the same questions—how can it be that such a great God would engage such flawed human beings.

I Corinthians 1:25-29:

> "Because the foolishness of God is wiser than men, and the weakness of God is stronger than men. For you see your calling, brethren, that not many wise according to the flesh, not many mighty, not many noble, are called. But God has chosen the foolish things of the world to put to shame the wise, and God has chosen the weak things of the world to put to shame the things which are mighty; and the base things of the world and the things which are despised God has chosen, and the things which are not, to bring to nothing the things that are, that no flesh should glory in His presence."

The answer is that it's okay to face the reality of our inadequacies. Doing so will bring us into a place of fully experiencing the all sufficiency of an Almighty God. As Moses' ministry progressed, he was on his face before God on more than a few occasions. He had learned to look up rather than to look down. He had accepted the fact that he couldn't do what God had called him to do without God's grace. We need to come to this place as well; it is God's way of showing the world and us, His grace, power and glory. So, embrace your insufficiency and experience God's great power.

What a privilege it is to be used by God to serve His people and His cause. It's an amazing opportunity and an incredibly rewarding experience. How awesome it is to

EMBRACE YOUR INSUFFICIENCY AND EXPERIENCE GOD'S GREAT POWER.

think that God actually called us to serve as His partners and allows us to do His bidding while wielding His great power.

We overcome our preoccupation with our inadequacies and walk boldly in our calling when we wholly comprehend His grace. We become free when we are able to see clearly that acting on behalf of God is not our own doing. God works through us as we yield ourselves to Him and he takes pleasure in doing so. Isn't that fantastic! I think it's important that we remind ourselves daily of this reality. When we do, it removes the weight of ministry from our shoulders and places it back where it belongs—onto His.

Reflecting on God's response to an inquiry that he had made, Paul said, *"...He said to me, 'My grace is sufficient for you, for My strength is made perfect in weakness.' Therefore most gladly I will rather boast in my infirmities, that the power of Christ may rest upon me"* (II Corinthians 12:9). Paul received the powerful revelation: When we are insufficient, the All-Sufficient One is able to shine so brightly through us.

The Ability to Serve

Perspective is everything. The thing that releases the power of God in our lives is a "yes" to his call, and a positive perspective. That's right, God is looking for people who will respond to Him in the affirmative. More than our know-how, years of experience, incredible resources, or connections, God desires willing workers. Then all of heaven's resources become available to us. It's important to note, however, that everything is tied to His schedule, not ours.

God gives us grace, divine enablement, supernatural ability, to serve His cause. It wasn't our resume that got us invited to the party. It's not because there is so much good in us, or that we were so brilliant. God, in His own counsel, elected to call us into divine partnership with Him even while we were blemished. We were born filled with His purpose!

Think of this in terms of a secular job. When an employee arrives at their place of employment, she doesn't have to dance and sing for the boss to get the equipment or supplies she needs. There will be no need to catch his eye or prove her loyalty to the company. The employee is simply required to do whatever job he or she was hired for. Everything else will be provided. If the person is a typist, a personal computer will be furnished; if a janitor, cleaning supplies will be furnished; if a pilot, a jet will be available.

In the kingdom of God, there is no difference. The work of the Church is the business of the King. God faithfully provides adequate resources to get His kingdom work done. You can fully expect God to supernaturally empower

---

YOU CAN FULLY EXPECT GOD TO SUPERNATURALLY EMPOWER YOU TO DO THE JOB HE HAS COMMISSIONED.

---

you to do the job He has commissioned you to do. No matter how large or small the task, God takes His business seriously. And, as with Moses, He will send co-laborers, having varying gifts, to covenant with you to finish the work He has called you to.

Divine Processing

God has deposited within the Body of Christ a myriad of gifts for the purpose of edification. Some are used to equip, others to help, and others to touch the world with His message. God entrusts us with our gifts and talents with the intent purpose of using them for His kingdom. However, it is ultimately our choice as to whether or not we will use them for His glory or for selfish purposes.

I have discovered that when we are born again, it is through the process of personal sanctification that our gifts are apprehended for the master's use. But God does not place His hand on our gifts to endorse, release, and

Leadership Essentials

prosper them until after He begins the process of personal transformation within us. Perhaps it's because without this process, pride is sure to rear its ugly head up. Just like Jacob, we first have to wrestle with God until we see Him alone as God. This keeps us from assuming the throne of our own lives once we experience the euphoria that comes with wielding His power.

In His Name

The world is not looking for you. It's not you that your church is looking for. It's God working in and through you. Consequently, your performance, image, or limited resources don't matter. Be like Moses: Give those who look to you the pure Word of God. Like Moses, remember that when you speak, you are no longer representing yourself. It's the great *I Am* who sends you. Therefore, you should never see yourself as autonomously going about doing the work of His ministry. You're representing the All-Powerful One, the King of kings, and Lord of lords. You have been given the authority to go in the powerful name of Jesus.

While working as a public relations practitioner prior to full-time ministry, I had the opportunity to work with some very powerful people, many of whom possessed great wealth and tremendous influence. When planning various business functions on their behalf, I would often go in their name as their representative. Even though I was the one present, because of the name of my client, the vendor would respond to me as if I was my client. I had been empowered to represent them. As a result, I entered their world of power and influence and could accomplish my clients' goals. There is nothing more intoxicating than walking in the name and authority of another.

But, here's a brief but significant word of caution: Don't allow success or the passing of time to lead you to believe that somehow this is about you. Someone once said that the donkey that heard the roar of the crowd while carrying Jesus during His triumphant entry thought for a minute that the cheers were for him. Moving about in His name is a powerful thing. But it's not about us; it's about the One who lives inside of us.

Increasing Grace

Supply meets demand. God responds to the calls of His people and has compassion for those who do not know Him. For this reason He will dispatch aid and assistance when there is a demand placed on heaven. Has it ever occurred to you that, just as with Moses, you could very well be the answer to someone's prayer?

I derive so much pleasure from observing people who comprehend the depth of what it means to serve in partnership with God, particularly those serving in areas that aren't the most celebrated. The greeter who bears a warm, welcoming smile; the custodian who takes great pride in keeping the house of God in order; the giver who knows the favor of God that has been granted to them and sows bountifully into the work of the kingdom. The more these people release themselves into the Master's service, the more God pours out in and through them.

When we realize that it is God who has placed us in our station in life, we function with humility, a much stronger resolve, and with a greater level of excellence. It is empowering when we understand the revelation that we have been given the grace to serve, and that what we are doing really does matter to God.

Entering Into His Rest

"Let us therefore be diligent to enter that rest, lest anyone fall according to the same example of disobedience"
(Hebrews 4:11).

The question of our ability must be settled in our own hearts. Without God we can do nothing. But with God all things are possible. We must press in to believe the Word of a faithful God who throughout the ages has taken insignificant men and women and accomplished incredible things. Remain convinced that the Lord will be strong on your behalf even on your worse days.

It is important to remind ourselves that the work God has called us to oversee is His church, His ministry and, more importantly, His idea. We must leave the burden with Him to fund, support, and give life to whatever He has established. Philippians 1:6 states, *"…being confident of this very thing, that He who has begun a good work in you will complete it until the day of Jesus Christ."*

I cannot tell you how many leaders I've seen who are forever stressed because they have taken ownership of something they've only been called to manage. However, even when we don't feel good about our gifts, talents, or present conditions of ministry, God is still faithful. He is faithful to His word and His cause. This is paramount to understand for our own mental, emotional and spiritual health. When you have given it all you've got, applied faith, and walked in obedience, it's time to let God be God. Remember, He alone gives the increase.

The battle begins and ends with our faith. T. L. Osborn, in his book [1]*Biblical Healing*, says, "Faith is expecting God to do what He promised." God calls us to fight the good fight of faith right to the finish, laboring to rest in His Word and His promises. It is through God's mighty power that we are able to achieve great things, all to His glory.

Will you dare believe today that God can accomplish much with the little that you bring to him? You must continue to preach the Word of grace to yourself. You can do what God has assigned you to do, because He empowers you daily to do so. You have been given grace to serve as an endowment, freely and without condition.

"Now to Him who is able to do exceedingly abundantly above all that we ask or think, according to the power that works in us" (Ephesians 3:20).

CHAPTER 3

THE NEED-TO-BE-NEEDED

For pastors, providing pastoral care to a congregation presents a unique set of complexities and potential hazards. The myriad of concerns dealt with during personal ministry can run the gamut from marriage and family matters, to addictive behavior and financial issues. Some are everyday life challenges, while others are more complicated. When providing aid and support to people, a bond of trust is

> **THE ABILITY TO TOUCH THE NEEDS OF OTHERS IS ALWAYS REWARDING, BUT FOR SOME IT CAN ALSO BE DANGEROUSLY INTOXICATING.**

established. This bond is critical to the healing process, but must also be kept in check by the caregiver. The ability to touch the needs of others is always rewarding, but for some it can also be dangerously intoxicating.

We know that, used correctly, legal drugs have many

beneficial purposes. However, abuse of the same can prove harmful; the extended use of a drug well after therapy has been completed will inevitably result in addiction. Likewise, helping other people is both good and honorable. But caregivers must know when enough is enough. Just like the continued use of a legal drug can lead to addiction, there is an unhealthy attachment that can develop between caregivers and those seeking their care, if either or both parties do not recognize the warning signs.

Moses learned a crucial lesson while attempting to deal with all the Israelites' interpersonal problems by himself. Jethro, his father-in-law, pulled him aside and instructed him with a bit of wisdom (see Exodus 18). He essentially told Moses that he was in over his head as he sat daily listening to the concerns of the people. It wasn't healthy for Moses, nor was it healthy for the Israelites. He needed to divide responsibility between others within the community who were also gifted to give wise counsel at varying levels.

Caregivers within a faith community—whether recognized leaders or laymen with the gift to administer healing, compassion, comfort, and assurance—are valuable to everyone. They love to see suffering people set free of their problems. They are nurturers and know how to reach the deep parts of a person's soul.

Mothers are a good example of caring nurturers. Tune in the television to a football game or some other sport and watch the parade of big brawny men waving at the camera, mouthing the words "Hi mom". It's not that dad is loved any less, but moms are valued on another level. For this reason it's virtually impossible to walk into a restaurant on Mother's Day without a reservation, but there is no problem finding an open seat on Father's Day. Like all nurturers, mothers are highly esteemed. The bottom line is that everyone loves a nurturer because of the way he/she makes us feel. Touching our souls, they minister to our self-esteem, our confidence, and to our overall sense of well being.

Nurturers are both needed and readily sought after in our faith communities. But caring for people requires discernment, wisdom, and self-control. Without these, something meant for good can prove to be injurious. It's easy to become enamored with the idea of people seeking us out. But we need to be careful of the *need-to-be-needed*. It is an unhealthy need that every caregiver must be aware of and careful to avoid; it can potentially afflict anyone having the responsibility or the heart to care for others, and lead to addiction.

The Ego Stroke

A root cause of the need-to-be-needed addiction is the desire for adoration and applause, the ego stroke. It feels good to be needed, and there are many who derive great satisfaction out of continually being sought after. I'm not suggesting that every caregiver helps out just to get his/her ego stroked. Dedication and selfless service to others should be recognized and celebrated. But for those who have a propensity toward this addiction, the attention may prove unhealthy because the applause can perpetuate the need. There are many people who fail to see this as a possible danger and are completely unaware of the risks.

For those who struggle with the need-to-be-needed, their serving extends beyond the simple satisfaction of seeing others restored. It has become a dependency. They have become the needy, needing to be needed by those they serve, and hunger to receive yet another call for their help.

The Needy

Those addicted to the need-to-be-needed are often highly motivated to do all they can to render aid to others in an effort to satisfy their compulsion. People suffering with this addiction are marked targets in congregations. Chronically needy people know who these caregivers are, and often prey on them, getting their attention fix met while also feeding the caregiver's addiction all in one stroke. Conversely, these caregivers often develop a following made up primarily of chronically needy and dysfunctional people. Between the needy and the caregiver, the addiction cycle is quickly set in motion and perpetuated every time they meet.

The congregation usually knows who the addicted are (although they might not label them as such), and will readily direct the hurting and needy their way. Those they send tend to be in a perpetual state of crisis. They have often refused to act responsibly to wise counsel previously given. Some refuse to make choices that will improve their situation, while others thrive off of the attention given to their ongoing problems.

Tough Times

"Many are the afflictions of the righteous, but the LORD delivers him out of them all" (Psalms 34:19).

When helping people, there are some realities we must face. A mature caregiver will risk appearing insensitive or uncaring and lead needy people to these realities. For instance, we all experience difficulties in this life. It's true that life just isn't fair and Christianity, contrary to the oversell, won't magically insulate us from problems. Nevertheless, Scripture does provide peace: *"And the peace of God, which surpasses all understanding, will guard your hearts and minds through Christ Jesus"* (Philippians 4:7). As well, Nehemiah 8:10 tells us that the joy of the Lord is our strength when we face difficulties. Although God is not the initiator of life's problems, they are used by Him to perfect us. Therefore, there are times when needy people should be left alone so that God can deal directly with their dilemmas. This requires wisdom on the part of the caregiver to know when to step in, and when to step back. By quickly running to the rescue, a caregiver can stand in the place of the Holy Spirit, hinder His working on behalf of the individual, and prolong their struggles. Doing so will prevent the person from dealing with their problems, and keep them from the benefits of the growth process that God has for them. As harsh as it may sound, wisdom tells us that it's unfair to rob anyone of God's growth process.

The Redirect

"Now to Him who is able to keep you from stumbling, And to present you faultless before the presence of His glory with exceeding joy, To God our Savior, Who alone is wise, Be glory and majesty, Dominion and power, Both now and forever Amen" (Jude 1:24-25).

Healthy ministry that deals with the needs of others won't have at its core a continuum of crisis. Yes there are times when crisis occurs, but these can be worked through

HEALTHY MINISTRY THAT DEALS WITH THE NEEDS OF OTHERS WON'T HAVE AT ITS CORE A CONTINUUM OF CRISIS.

within a reasonable time frame, if God's wisdom is used. The problem comes in when the need-to-be-needed addiction feeds on the crisis. It's important to do away with the 911 mentality. Crisis simply provides another occasion to experience the rush and euphoria of coming to the rescue of yet another needy soul, while feeding the addiction.

When providing pastoral care, the objective is to direct believers towards their ultimate source of help, Jesus Christ. We must be careful to avoid any level of dependency upon us to be established. Our role is to aid the person in becoming healthy and fully reliant upon their Heavenly Father.

THE OBJECTIVE IS TO DIRECT BELIEVERS TOWARDS THEIR ULTIMATE SOURCE OF HELP, JESUS CHRIST.

Lone Rangers

One of many consequences of needing to be needed is the lone ranger syndrome. The lone ranger progressively becomes an island unto himself. They rarely seek to distribute the load they carry or defer to others who may be better equipped to handle a particular problem. It is often clear they are beyond their ability, their scope of responsibility, and in many cases, their authority. If left alone long enough, it becomes difficult for these people to relate properly to a team concept or submit to authority.

Jesus said, *"I and my father are one."* Unity is first and foremost demonstrated within the Godhead (John 10:30). And Jesus is the perfect model of submission to authority. How is it that we think we can be fruitful without working in concert under the authority of God and the authority set in place in the earth? We can't! Family, community, covenant–team is a God idea and it works to bring God's purposes to fruition.

There are many biblical models of teams that work. Solomon writes that two are better than one. Moses and Aaron exemplify team ministry. Jesus sent the disciples out in twos. Within the context of community, there is

> **THERE IS NO ROOM FOR THE LONE RANGER.**

no room for the lone ranger. With teams, there is shared gifting, and a sharing of knowledge, insights, responsibility, and safety. The team can serve to protect a caregiver from going it alone, becoming isolated and ultimately becoming a danger to someone else or themselves.

"Where no counsel is, the people fall: but in the multitude of counselors there is safety" (Proverbs 11:14).

Telltale Signs

Here are a few telltale signs that indicate that you may suffer from the need-to-be-needed.
- You think you are the only one who can solve the problem or situation.
- Calls come into your home at inappropriate times.
- You frequently and *justifiably* neglect your family to attend to the needs of others.
- There is the tendency to gather needy followers unto yourself.
- You feel that *you* must always be there for the needy.
- You frequently allow your personal time and space to be invaded by the needy.
- Inquiries are made regarding the well being of those *you* regularly *counsel.*

Serving Healthy

Whether you already know that you suffer from this addiction or are just becoming aware that you may be in this position, you can take precautions to protect yourself by following these guidelines:

- Point people to God.
- Pray for God's wisdom in serving His people. Always maintain the position that we all belong to Him, and we are His ultimate responsibility.
- Being diligent as a caregiver.
- Establish systems of accountability. Start with your pastor. If you don't have one, get one.
- Learn when and how to say no. You are not God's only answer to every needy person's problem.
- Establish clear boundaries and set parameters that will protect everyone involved.
- Honestly and regularly assess how your ministry to others is affecting your family and/or your personal time.
- Always place a stated limit on the time you will spend listening to or caring for others, for their benefit and yours. Most professionals suggest no more than an hour for each session.
- Be careful not to allow empathy (putting yourself in their position and feeling their hurt) to pull you too far into the person's struggle.
- When faced with difficult challenges, be honest with the individual seeking aid. Let them know when a particular problem is beyond your ability, experience or authority. Don't try to be everything to everyone.
- Whenever you find yourself in over your head, get help, and hand off.

The gift of compassion and caring is both needed and greatly valued. When properly appropriated it can bring healing and restoration. Submit your gift to God, walk in wisdom and experience the blessing of being a blessing.

CHAPTER 4

THE PRIDE FACTOR

"And whoever exalts himself will be humbled, and he who humbles himself will be exalted" (Matthew 23:12).

God has a tremendous purpose for your life and it is important to guard the journey toward your destiny. In this chapter, I want to specifically address pride as it relates to destiny, knowing that our destiny will only be fully realized if pursued according to God's kingdom principles.

Gloria and I were once on a beach in the Caribbean taking photos of the island's beauty. I had a neat little Pentax camera that my brother had given me as a gift. I really loved taking pictures with this camera; I had become so familiar with it and the images were always so crisp. Upon returning home I'd discovered that a grain of sand had made its way into the camera's viewfinder. I shook the camera, disassembled it, and blew air into every possible crevice in an attempt to remove that grain of sand, to no avail. Later, the thought occurred to me that pride operates in our lives in exactly the same way. No matter how hard we try to rid ourselves of it, it still remains. I am convinced that we are all contaminated with the sin of pride on some level. However, we must continue to eliminate it whenever it shows up, and to pursue humility, as it is the key to kingdom advancement.

Reducing the pride factor leads to success in life and in God's kingdom. This principle runs in stark contrast to the kingdoms of this world. In the world, those who walk in humility are perceived to be weak, defenseless, and lacking tenacity. If we want to be successful in life, dependence upon self is necessary, or so it is believed. Not so in God's

REDUCING THE PRIDE FACTOR LEADS TO SUCCESS IN LIFE AND IN GOD'S KINGDOM.

kingdom. The way to the top is to realize we were born dependent. Dependence upon God and interdependence on others brings us ultimate success. God does not call us to be an island unto ourselves, and there is a pride factor that comes in when people say, "God is all I need too."

Second Timothy 3:4 states that the day would come when men would be, *"traitors, headstrong, haughty, lovers of pleasure rather than lovers of God."* The word haughty that is used in this verse comes from a Greek word which means *to be enveloped in smoke.* Like smoke, one of the things that pride does is to distort our view, making it impossible for us to see correctly.

The Pride Factor

When Satan succumbed to pride, he became completely self-centered. It blinded him and induced self-importance. Pride produced a *god complex* within his mind causing him to think that he was in control and that he could overthrow the government of heaven. Where did it land him? In failure and ultimately in the lake of fire; he will never fulfill his created purpose.

Kingdom success isn't automatic just because we're busy doing things in the name of the Lord. Unfortunately many people operate under this pretense. We need to understand there are conditions and mindsets produced by pride that act like a cancer in the divine plan of God for our lives. We must recognize pride when we see it, own up to it, and take action against it. One of the most damaging things that pride does is to create a chasm between our needs and the ability to see the answer to them. I see *need* as God's personal pride-o-meter for us.

Let's take a look at the story of Naaman found in II Kings 5. This powerful man was commander of the Syrian army. But the story reveals how pride can hinder the blessings and provisions of God in our lives and potentially prevent us from reaching our destiny. The Bible says that Naaman was a great and honorable man in the eyes of his king and a man of valor. Wouldn't we all like to be held in such high esteem? He was also a leper and that's not something you nor I would want to have on our resume. Most likely, he would have been ostracized from his society, because of the social stigma that leprosy carried. It's also possible this disease hindered his ability to adequately perform his military duties.

Naaman needs a miracle; there was no cure for leprosy. And God was going to provide one for him. Before receiving it, however, there were several encounters that he needed to face. These encounters placed Naaman's pride on display and provide us with a vivid picture of its injurious affects.

God first used a young captive Israelite girl who had become Namaan's wife's maid. Seeing Naaman's condition and how miserable it made his life, her faith in God moved her to tell of a prophet who could heal him. At a time when the voice of a women wasn't considered credible, God used this young maiden to point Namaan towards divine aid. It is possible that he may have been reluctant to receive this information considering its source. However, he may also have chosen to listen to her because he was in the privacy of his own home. Prideful people often find it easier to receive information in private rather than in public.

Petitioning the king for a release, Naaman told him about the prophet Elisha residing in Samaria, who had the power to heal him. The king granted his request, sending him and his travel companions off with diplomatic letters authorizing their travel and mission. No doubt Naaman thought, "Surely the king's blessings would afford him additional clout and preferential treatment."

After he arrives in town, he is taken to Elisha's house. He and his entourage pull up outside fully expecting a formal reception and swift response to his request. Instead, Elisha sends out a messenger with these directions: *"Go, wash yourself seven times in the Jordan, and your flesh will be restored and you will be cleansed"* (verse ten). Insulted, Naaman becomes furious because Elisha refuses to come out to greet him as a man of great stature.

Point number one: When in need, there is no place for pride. Put it away. I recently read some news stories of Hollywood stars checking into chic rehab facilities to

WHEN IN NEED, THERE IS NO PLACE FOR PRIDE.

---

overcome their addictions. Many would return again and again, never really making any progress. During a recent television interview, actor and former child star, Todd Bridges said, "the last thing you need when you're in rehab is to be treated like a star." Proverbs 16:18 states, *"Pride goes before destruction, a haughty spirit before a fall."* Attack pride whenever you see it in your life, and keep humility in the forefront of your mind: it always has its place no matter who you are or what your status is in life.

In pursing the things of God, we must be open to receive on His terms. Our pride will lead us to specify the conditions under which we are willing to see our needs met and to receive our supply. However, names, titles and achievements are of no consequence when we are lacking.

PRIDE WILL LEAD US TO SPECIFY THE CONDITIONS UNDER WHICH WE ARE WILLING TO SEE OUR NEEDS MET.

At the end of the day, what's most important is that we get what God has for us so we can continue walking toward our destiny.

Back to our story. Naaman didn't need to be honored; he needed a miraculous healing. As if dishonoring him before his entire convoy wasn't enough, Elisha next sends a messenger to tell him to bathe in the Jordan. The Jordan of all places—another insult! And, not just once, but he was told to bathe seven times. Enraged, Naaman departs Elisha's house, refusing to be humiliated any farther.

I Corinthians 1:27-29 states:

> *"...God has chosen the foolish things of the world to put to shame the wise, and God has chosen the weak things of the world to put to shame the things which are mighty; and the base things of the world and the things which are despised God has chosen, and the things which are not, to bring to nothing the things that are, that no flesh should glory in His presence."*

There are so many instances in scripture where seemingly nonsensical things are used to bring healing and deliverance to God's people. Elijah experienced catered meals from a raven; Gideon was told to reduce the number of soldiers in his army in order to conquer the enemy; Jesus was born in a manger; the disciples were purported to be unlearned; and one man was even healed when Jesus used his own spit to make mud, then placed it on the man's eyes. These were all humiliating experiences that led to a miraculous event.

It was God who directed Elisha to tell Namaan to dip seven times in the muddy waters of the Jordan in order to be healed. Besides healing him, God also wanted to deal with the pride factor in Naaman's life. Then God alone

PRIDE IS ONE OF THOSE THINGS THAT GETS BURIED DEEP DOWN IN OUR HEARTS.

would get the glory and His limitless power would be clearly established in Naaman's heart.

Like the grain of sand that ruined my camera, pride is one of those things that gets buried deep down in our hearts. God commandeers life's circumstances and conditions to drive those hidden, prideful "grains of sand" to the surface.

When I started my church, it was humiliating to think that my survival depended on the selfless giving of those I served. I had been an entrepreneur all of my life; independence was my middle name. During the formative years of ministry, it was awkward to receive gifts such as

WE HINDER THE FLOW OF GOD'S BLESSINGS WHEN WE ALLOW PRIDE TO BLOCK THE DOOR OF HIS CHOSEN WAYS OF PROVISION.

food, assistance with vacations, or clothes for my children. I had been accustomed to making things happen on my own, even if it meant I would struggle. God used those experiences to increase my faith, reduce the pride factor in my life, and to show me how to receive His provisions on His terms. I'm convinced God will never leave us without our needs met. However, we hinder the flow of God's blessings when we allow pride to block the door of His chosen ways of provision.

In Naaman's case, God uses yet another servant to minister to him (it's important to note that God's true servants will speak beneficial truth to us, even if it bruises our egos. If we are able to discern correctly through the smoke of our own pride, we will recognize that their motives are

TRUE SERVANTS WILL SPEAK BENEFICIAL TRUTH TO US, EVEN IF IT BRUISES OUR EGOS.

clear and without malice). Namaan's servant had the loving audacity to direct Naaman back to the road of humility so that he could receive his miracle. The servant was led by the Holy Spirit to respectfully show him his arrogance, while encouraging him to pursue what God had sent him there to receive. *"And his servants came near and spoke to him, and said, 'My father, if the prophet had told you to do something great, would you not have done it? How much more then, when he tells you, 'Wash, and be cleansed'!"* (verse thirteen). Naaman went down and dipped seven times in the Jordan, and his flesh was restored like the flesh of a little child. Albeit a bit delayed, Naaman's willingness to swallow his pride would not only bring him physical healing, but salvation as well.

Many leaders have missed their ministry provisions because they refuse to allow God to deal with their pride factor. It is true that no man is an island. We need the gifting, direction, wisdom and substance of others. Let those who God sends your way blow the smoke of your pride from your eyes so that you can experience God's fullness for your life.

A Community Design

The church, by God's design, is a community. The word *church* has its origins in the Greek word *Koinonia*, which means partnership or fellowship, and carries the basic idea of having things in common. We are in divine partnership with God and one another. We are all in this together for the same reason—to bring glory to the name of our Lord Jesus Christ. We were created to enjoy all of the blessings of communal living. God hates pride because true Koinonia or community cannot be achieved when pride is present. We can never reach our fullest potential and destiny as long as we allow pride to thwart God's plans and provision for our lives. Pride produces isolation, self-centeredness, competitiveness, and territorialism. It also gives us a mindset of ignorance, a false sense of security, and ultimately insufficiency.

Bringing Down the Pride Factor

Dealing with your pride will be a life-long pursuit. Start by being honest with God and yourself. When you see the ugly sin of pride rising up, confess it to God right away.

One of the best ways to know when pride is at work in our lives is through the honest, loving words of someone we respect. An accountability partner is priceless. These relationships are God given and takes time to develop. It's a matter of finding someone who wants what you want, to be pleasing to the Lord.

Take action

- Let God's glory be your continued focus.
- Practice being vulnerable.
- Know who you are and accept who you are not.
- Recognize your shortcomings and accept them *(we're not omni-anything)*.
- Reach out for help to fill your weak spots.
- Recognize, value, and celebrate the gifts and talents of others.
- Refuse to be isolated.
- Network and build fruitful relationships.
- Become intentional about tearing down the strongholds of:
  Fear
  Old paradigms
  Tradition
  Competition
  Self-centeredness
  Territorialism
  Insecurity
  Independence

The Pride Factor

First Peter 5:6-7: *"Therefore humble yourselves under the mighty hand of God, that He may exalt you in due time, casting all your care upon Him, for He cares for you."*

CHAPTER 5

REDEFINING SUCCESS

Success – it is the measurable result of a planned effort and one of the most sought after things in life. Entrepreneurs work diligently to see their ventures turn a profit, parents raise their children with the hope they will become successful in life, and in Christian circles, leaders in ministry want to build congregations that will make a difference.

While we all long to be successful, what defines success varies from person to person; it is highly subjective. In my case, before entering full-time ministry, I was an entrepreneur here in Chicago. As the head of my own public relations firm, I spent some fifteen years pursuing entrepreneurial success. Then in 1990, while in my late 20s, the U. S. Small Business Administration recognized me as Illinois' Young Entrepreneur of the Year. It was a proud moment for my family and me. It wasn't largesse or massive amounts of money that motivated me; I was more thrilled with the idea of being in the game of big business, being in control of my own destiny and creating opportunities where none had existed. I also prided myself on delivering an excellent end product for my clients. This brought me fulfillment and had become my measure of success.

What I'd discovered, however, is that measuring success differed among fellow entrepreneurs. Many were driven entirely by the idea of building a big business, amassing more money, more toys and notoriety. For others, climbing the social ladder or growing in political clout became their measure of success. Sadly, these are also the standards often used in the Christian world. I believe today the church—and in particular, Christian leadership—is in desperate need of a biblical definition for success.

Over the past ten years my wife, Gloria, and I have served together as leaders in a ministry that we planted together, Harvest Church Plainfield, in suburban Chicago. We started the church with seven adults and our children; it was a challenging experience, but extremely rewarding. To give you an idea of the struggles we faced, in the beginning months Gloria and I would drive home arguing over who would run over the other with the car when we arrived home. It was our way of humorously dulling the pain of a difficult process. Nevertheless, the idea that we were living by faith and clearly walking toward our destiny sustained us during the formative years.

When we first announced the start of our ministry, many people spoke words of affirmation over us. Some said, "You'll grow overnight," others commented, "There will be thousands following you." It was assumed that success in business would automatically translate into instant success in ministry. We felt pressured to pursue this idea of success and allow their definitions to become our definition. And, as we all know, it feels so good to have people pointing to us, speaking about us in glowing terms, celebrating our intelligence, applauding our ability to move crowds, and build great structures. The thought of it can be so intoxicating. However, as a discipline, whenever a word was spoken over us, I would graciously thank the person for their vote of confidence. But in my heart I was determined not to allow their comments to influence what I believed was God's idea of ministry success.

In the years following the initial startup of Harvest, my itinerate ministry beyond our home church has allowed me to interact with Christian leaders from various denominations. Some of these leaders have achieved success on a number of levels: They serve thousands of members and have constructed incredible structures, while others have just a handfull of followers and are in rented facilities. When talking ministry with these wonderful, well meaning brothers and sisters, often their focus has been on the size of congregations, the size of facilities, and how quickly everything developed. Someone would ask, "Hey McCants, how many you running out there? Did you build yet?" These questions made it easy to feel that I might be doing something wrong. Without being clear on what kingdom success is, it is easy to leave this sort of meeting, feeling like a wanna-be, hoping for the day to experience *real* success like the "big boys." Increasingly, my frustration heightened because nobody asked pertinent questions like, how has your community been impacted by your ministry? How many people have you seen move from infancy to maturity? or, Are you seeing the uninformed come to know God?

From the start I've been careful not to become preoccupied with counting heads or dollars. Gloria says she believes the Lord placed blinders on me in the early years of ministry. Although there were many Sundays when fewer than ten people were present, I preached as though there were thousands. I had set my heart on warring against what I believed to be a shallow measurement of ministry success. We can't quantify what God is doing by what we see with our eyes; His mathematics are not the same as ours, which is why we must discipline ourselves to walk by faith, not by sight. Harvest Church Plainfield has experienced growth over the years, not in the thousands, but a few hundreds have joined our sweet little faith community. We are grateful to God for bringing us all together so that we can help in expanding His kingdom.

Proper Judgment

Judgment is defined by how a matter is viewed, one's opinion, and the proper determination of its place. In the process, the measurement used to judge is the key. By what

BY WHAT SET OF VALUES DO YOU JUDGE OR DETERMINE SUCCESS?

set of values do you judge or determine success? Proverbs 14:12 states, *"There is a way that seems right to a man, but its end is the way of death"* (NKJV). There is obviously another way—God's way—that is right and leads to life filled with abundance.

The problem is that the church has been guilty of judging things in life with the same measure that the world uses. In some cases these judgments are made in an effort to relate to the world, but more often than not they are made to satisfy an uncontrolled worldly appetite for material things. As a consequence, we find ourselves falling into the traps that come with pursuing created things rather than

THE CHURCH HAS BEEN GUILTY OF JUDGING THINGS IN LIFE WITH THE SAME MEASURE THAT THE WORLD USES.

the Creator, *"straying from the faith in greediness, and piercing ourselves through with many sorrows"* (I Timothy 6:10 NKJV). Some of these piercings include family breakdowns and divorce, imprisonment for financial improprieties, moral failure, and a dangerous preoccupation with the temporal. We need proper judgment in order to produce fruit that means success in the economy of the kingdom.

Influenced

For those of us in full-time ministry, we need to ask ourselves: What measurable results qualify as kingdom success? What meets kingdom agenda and pleases our

Father? We know that the world measures success by quantity, volume and mass, bigger, better, more. This philosophy is not new; it is recorded in the book of Genesis: And they said, *"Come, let us build ourselves a city, and a tower whose top is in the heavens; let us make a name for ourselves..."* (Genesis 11:4 NKJV). Yet Christians today have the same mentality; we have become fully convinced that abundance and making a name for ourselves—particularly as it relates to tangible things—equals success.

It is common today to see import cars, airplanes, houses and large centers for worship highlighted during the opening of Christian television programs or prominently displayed in ministry publications. Sadly, these have become the symbols of our success. Yes, there are certain things needed to expand the influence and reach God's kingdom on the earth. I want it to be clear that I am not in any way suggesting that land, buildings, money, and other resources aren't needed, nor is it a sin to have and enjoy them. But there is an appropriate place and use for them all, and material things need to be kept in proper perspective. These should be viewed as a means to an end, not a goal to be attained.

[2]Tommy Barnett in his book, *Hidden Power,* says, *"There's a place in God where we can ask for anything and receive it. But the key to finding that place is asking for something that is consistent with His heart. Get inside His mind; get Him inside of you, and then you begin to think as He does. His desires fuse with yours, and you no longer want to ask for Rolls Royces and mansions – you want to ask for food for the hungry. Your desires become like God's desires."*

Matthew 6:33 tells us to seek first God's kingdom and to do things that will bring praise to Him, according to His ways and His purposes, pursuing righteousness every step of the way. When we do so, everything needed to accomplish His wishes and meet our needs will be given to us. Imagine, as we follow His leading, we are freely given all things needed to build the church (His body) so that people everywhere will come into a right relationship with God.

Kingdom Success

The war we're engaged in is far too critical to allow ourselves to be anesthetized by a pseudo success based on materialism. Real kingdom success is based on fruitfulness, a word we've heard from the garden forward (see also Mark 4: 1-20). It was a mandate given in Genesis and the measure of a successful disciple in the gospels. John 15:8 (NKJV): *"By this My Father is glorified, that you bear much fruit; so you will be My disciples."*

REAL KINGDOM SUCCESS IS BASED ON FRUITFULNESS.

It's not the process of constructing ministry that impresses God; it is the net result, fruitfulness that does. Kingdom success is not gauged by the impressive building we erect, but what happens to the people inside them and how these same people influence the world they live in. It's not how many we seat over the weekend; it's how many become disciples and grow in maturity to become fruitful laborers.

> The church has three primary functions in the world:
> 1) To proclaim the gospel message and serve as purveyors of hope for the hopeless and uninformed.
> 2) To equip the believer to become functioning citizens of God's Kingdom.
> 3) To serve as a distinctive community made up of dynamic influencers modeling Christ throughout society.

In Matthew five, Jesus describes the church as being salt and light. These speak of undeniable influence and the preservation of righteousness. As we increasingly cooperate with God in all areas of our lives, everything within our reach will be impacted for the kingdom of God and the gates of hell will not prevail. When the mature church rises and takes her rightful place, there will be such a contrast between righteousness and evil, and light and darkness that the world will run into Zion seeking answers. At the end of the day the kingdoms or systems of the world will all have to bow to the King of kings and Lord of lords. Revelations 11:15 says: *"Then the seventh angel sounded: And there were loud voices in heaven, saying, 'The kingdoms of this world have become the **kingdoms** of our Lord and of His Christ, and He shall reign forever and ever!'"* That spells true success.

The Distinctions

There are two systems constantly pressuring us everyday, influencing us, intent on securing our devotion. These are the Kingdom of God *(the place of Christ's sovereignty where things are done according to His ways)* and the kingdoms of this world *(the perversion of the former, established by the enemy to rob God of His glory and ensnare God's people)*. The first comes to us *by* invitation and *with* our cooperation, while the latter *forces* its way upon us through demand and pressure.

The following are two lists of characteristics describing these opposing kingdoms. As you seek to discern which of these systems are vying for your allegiance, these might be helpful in your making an accurate determination about what you consider to be true success. Remember, love is the guiding principle of the Kingdom of God, while lust is the signature of the kingdoms of this world.

The pursuit of success according to world systems produces:
Anxiety
Frustration
Impatience
Manipulation
A competitive spirit
Territorialism
A preoccupation with quantity
An insatiable thirst for more things
The fear of loss

Pride
An attitude of ownership
The spirit of a pimp
(people being a means to an end)

The pursuit of success according to the Kingdom of God produces:
Obedience
Integrity
Diligence
Humility
Faithfulness
A desire to bring God glory
Spirit of a servant and steward
Selflessness
Expectation that God alone provides
Righteousness, peace and Joy in the Holy Spirit

It's His Church

Deuteronomy 8:17-18 (NKJV): *"then you say in your heart, 'My power and the might of my hand have gained me this wealth.' 18 "And you shall remember the LORD your God, for it is He who gives you power to get wealth, that He may establish His covenant which He swore to your fathers, as it is this day."*

While we have been commissioned to build the world-wide church—which embodies believers everywhere—we do so as stewards under God's authority, not owners wielding sovereign powers. The servant who experiences the most joy is the same one who fully realizes it is God's church, purchased by the blood of Jesus Christ. This important revelation will cause us to continually return to God for sustenance rather than toward our own limitations. II Corinthians 9:8 (NKJV): *"And God is able to make all grace abound toward you, that you, always having all sufficiency in all things, may have an abundance for every good work."*

Furthermore, we must realize that it is far more important to God that we succeed in our commission than it is to us; His intent is to present to Himself a glorious church (Ephesians 5:27). Remember Philippians 2:13 (NKJV) states, *"it is God who works in you both to will and to do for His good pleasure."* Heaven is pulling for all of us.

When Gloria and I began planning for our church, I stated in a meeting that we would never consider going into a school because it would be too obscure. What happened? We found ourselves in a high school for over seven years. But God wasn't finished showing us how He works through the obscure, undesirable and unattractive to bring glory to His name. Our next church location was in the basement of an office building—in a building behind a building at that! Granted, it the best-looking basement we have ever seen. After nearly ten years God granted us favor, giving us a prime piece of land and moving on the heart of an affluent friend to loan our church a substantial amount (at a lower than market rate) to close the deal. There was no anxiety, fear of loss, frustration or need for manipulation, but a knowing that this is God's church and, as I shared with our congregation, when He gets tired of His church being in a basement, then He'll move it. In the meantime, if

He's happy, then we should be content. Does this mean we had taken a nonchalant attitude over the years? Not at all! We've pursued every lead and knocked on every possible door looking for a yes in due season. But through it all we rested in knowing that in His time, the needs and resources would intersect. And, that they did!

Suggestions to Help You Achieve True Kingdom Success:

Develop your ministry based on a biblically sound definition of success and be disciplined to live by it. Measure all that you do by the Word and you won't be moved by fads and popular opinion (Joshua 1:8).

Guard your heart by choosing your ministry acquaintances carefully (Proverbs 13:20, Psalms 119:62).

Write out your vision, test it by truth, and refer to it often.

Invite a person of integrity to serve as your accountability partner. Give him/her the license to be in-your-face-honest (Proverbs 27:6).

Beware of flattering lips (Proverbs 26:28).

Judge your own heart and motives first, and then present your struggles to the Lord (I Corinthians 11:28-31).

Redefining Success

"*The steps of a good man are ordered by the LORD, And He delights in his way*" (Psalms 37:23 NKJV).[1]

CHAPTER 6

CREATING CULTURE

As a kid growing up in suburban Chicago, it wasn't uncommon to see people walking down the street on their way to church, dressed in their Sunday best. I can vividly recall seeing the bright springtime dresses, white lacy hats, and fathers proudly accompanying their families to church. It was a simple time when Sunday mornings were sacred, and everyone knew what to expect from the worship experience. There would be no multimedia presentation, no dramas, or food courts. Most churches had Sunday School, music, a message, and a brief time of fellowship afterwards. Denominations were strong back then, and you could travel throughout America and find an affiliate church with a similar culture.

Because of the familiarity and commonality created by denominations, people rarely changed. I remember hearing statements like, "I was born a Baptist and I'll die a Baptist." There are families who for generations have held to the traditions of a particular denomination. This incredible loyalty was birthed out of a common belief, common purpose, but mostly familiarity.

In many churches today, this has all changed. The neighborhood church as we once knew it is fading. Loyalty to a particular denomination is no longer the case. Instead of walking, people now travel for miles to worship at a church where they feel they fit in. People shop for churches like they're shopping for a mini van. There are thousands of churches emerging without any affiliation to a mainline denomination. With so many options, it is becoming difficult for church leaders to determine why people are attending their particular ministry. With the emergence of the so-called "independent church" there is no longer an advantage to the branding that came with a denominational affiliation. This makes it more challenging to promote the distinctiveness of a particular church; it is a point of frustration for many church leaders, but it doesn't have to be. It's a matter of becoming more sophisticated in our approach to ministry so that we reach out to a more sophisticated population. We are not called to cater to their needs per se. It's more about knowing who we are as leaders, what we offer in our ministry, then clearly communicating our vision on a number of levels.

I have mentioned the word *culture* several times. Webster's Dictionary defines *culture* as "the characteristic features of everyday existence shared by people in a place or

CULTURE IS THE COLLECTIVE WAY WE DO WHAT WE DO.

---

time; the set of shared attitudes, values, goals, and practices that characterizes an institution or organization." Simply put, culture is the collective way we do what we do.

For a church congregation—and by extension, the Body of Christ as a whole—the foundation of our culture is our theology—how we view God, His creation, the Church or life itself. It's all wrapped up in what we believe. Your church's culture determines who will join you and become a part of your church's mission, and who will look elsewhere. Not that you would want to drive anyone away;

> **WHEN VALUES AND EXPECTATIONS DON'T MEET, THERE IS NO FOUNDATION UPON WHICH TO ESTABLISH A MEANINGFUL RELATIONSHIP.**

it's just a reality that when values and expectations don't meet, there is no foundation upon which to establish a meaningful relationship.

Jesus was known to cut to the chase and pre-qualify those seeking to join him in His mission. For instance, a certain scribe approached him. *"Teacher, I will follow You wherever You go."* And Jesus said to him, *"Foxes have holes and birds of the air have nests, but the Son of Man has nowhere to lay His head."* Then another of His disciples said to Him, *"Lord, let me first go and bury my father."* But Jesus said to him, *"Follow Me, and let the dead bury their own dead"* (Matthew 8:19-22). Jesus clearly articulated His values to these men and quickly helped them make a decision. Apparently they did not share Jesus' values. Depending on your vision or even its stage of development, you will find those that will be unwilling to walk with you. The sooner you know who is with you, the better it will be for all involved. This will greatly help you in accomplishing what God has called you to do. Jesus was pursuing the cross and had no room for excess baggage, and the truth is that neither do we if we want to "run the race" that God has called us to.

Building Multi-Culturally

There are many churches desiring to build a multicultural congregation, which is commendable, and I believe the heart of our Lord. Doing so requires leadership that understands and fully comprehends the dynamic power of culture. People gather where they feel comfortable with those of like-minds, having shared values, experiences, and identities. My ministry has managed to retain what I would call a good representation of cross cultures. Since our inception, we have enjoyed a mix of African American, Caucasian, Asian, and Latin American members. We are constantly working to develop ways to create an environment where anyone can determine for themselves whether or not they feel at home. It's not easy, but it's worth it. Our expectation is to have a place where there is harmony between all.

A Deliberate Approach

The culture of your church can be the result of one of two things: you can have a deliberate planned strategy to create culture, or there can be the more common culture that comes about without thought, plan, or intent. It just evolves.

In 2003, I was blessed with the opportunity to travel to the capital city of Abuja in Nigeria, Africa. It was my first missionary trip to Africa. I noticed there were new roads being laid and new buildings under construction. Our team even had the opportunity to tour a massive Ecumenical Centre. Now complete, it's a facility used for major Christian meetings. During our time there, I was told that Lagos, the former capital of Nigeria, had evolved too fast for the infrastructure to accommodate the growth and traffic of this bustling metropolis. Abuja, on the other hand, is a planned city, one that the government had painstakingly cultivated, considering every detail for present and future growth and development.

Most often a church's culture is a mosaic of a dominant leader's beliefs, preferences and experiences, as well as those who have become members. It can be a collection of ideas and concepts, traditions, fears and beliefs that may or may not be valid. In this case, very little strategic forethought has gone into the process of creating culture and how it will impact the development of the Ministry. In the case of the larger umbrella or denominational organization, culture is very often adopted or inherited. The values and traditions of these organizations are firmly held to and carefully

THE IDEAL SCENARIO IS A WELL
THOUGHT-OUT STRATEGIC PLAN THAT WILL
CREATE CULTURE.

guarded, even when they work against the health of the organization.

The ideal scenario is a well thought-out strategic plan that will create culture on purpose and cause the God-breathed vision for your unique faith community to come to fruition. And of course the best culture is a Bible-based culture.

The first thing we must realize is that culture is screaming out at those we are seeking to engage, whether or not we are consciously aware of it. Our culture is expressed in so many ways. It surfaces in forms of worship. It is heard in our language. Our choices of music, literature, dress, and our display of or lack of public emotion speaks of our culture. Even our architecture and design of our worship facilities states who we are and what is important to our group.

Creating culture is a matter of getting in touch with the heart of God concerning your ministry. Sometimes this is difficult, as our closeness to the vision is very much akin to not being able to see the forest for the trees. You can begin by asking yourself several questions. These questions may also be asked of those who make up your core group.

- What specifically do you believe God has planted your ministry in the world to achieve? Why does your ministry even exist? Remember your ministry is unique and its purpose for being is unlike any other.

- What are we extremely passionate about? What is it that wakes us in the morning, and puts us to sleep late at night? What is it that we would do even if we never received payment or recognition?
- What aspect of ministry continues to surface as a main focus?

Every ministry has a specific emphasis. For some it will be developing and empowering the believer for service, while for others it might be Sunday School and children. Then there are those churches whose idea of successful ministry is touching their community. Every ministry is unique and God has given each a specific mandate.

Being in touch with your ministry's mandate is paramount to the process of creating culture. At our church, we place a strong emphasis on equipping the believer for the work of ministry according to Ephesians chapter

VISION IS NOT WHAT YOU SEE OTHERS DO.

four. As a result, we frequently refer to our church as an equipping station. We expect those who become members of our congregation to be actively involved in touching the world with the gospel of the kingdom both in word and demonstration. We want to be salt and light in the world.

As you conduct this self examination, consider the unique qualities of your ministry. Perhaps you are strong in music and the arts. Or maybe your strength is in evangelism strategies. It might be that your ministry appeals to young people. These unique qualities point to your ministry's purpose for being—the unique vision that God has for your church. It is a reflection of God's grace upon your faith community. I've met too many leaders who did not have a clear idea of their ministry's purpose. When asked about their vision, they are vague at best.

Remember, vision is not what you see others do. Nor is it necessary that your ministry follows the pattern of what you've seen before. We have far too many copycat ministries. I have great respect and admiration for the fathers in the gospel who have trained and groomed me for ministry. And while their wisdom and example has provided a great foundation and continues to minister to me, I've never feared venturing out and employing new methods of conducting ministry.

You must allow God to develop a sense of adventure in and through you. He is still looking for those who will freely and boldly flow in his creative and diverse nature. He has not called you to be a politician, but a leader. The church is not a democracy, it's a theocracy. Daring to be different is not a sin, so give yourself license to dismiss some old traditions and establish some new ones. God's vision for your ministry is tailored to your church.

There are several organizational tools needed to help you maintain the continuity and integrity of your vision. These are:
- A mission statement

- A vision statement
- List of core values
- A creed

It is important that your leadership and the entire church membership understand each of these items and how they relate to one another. You must be disciplined to refer back to them often, to help keep the ministry focused and on course. These things should be clearly reflected in every area of your ministry; there should be a direct correlation between your proclamation and demonstration.

Because there are so many needs in the world, it is easy to become sidetracked and find yourself stepping into areas that are unrelated to your mission. You'll then find yourself expending resources, human and otherwise, which ultimately detract from the reason God wanted you to plant your church. Stay focused! These tools will help you if properly developed and employed.

Mission Statement

In his book, [3]*The Power of Vision*, George Barna states that a *mission statement* is a broad-based definition of the reason for existing. It should under gird everything your church does and stands for. At Harvest our vision is three-pronged: We want to creatively introduce the gospel locally and world-wide, strengthen the local body, and serve as a resource to the body of Christ. My church supports my efforts to write the book you are now reading, because the members know that it is part of our vision. We are a resource to the Body.

You can even ask one of the children in children's ministry and they will tell you what our mission is.

Vision Statement

A *vision statement* is more specific. It details what your ministry will look like in the future. I think this can be powerfully motivating. It describes such things as the sort of ministries you will establish, the types of buildings you will construct, the culture and people you will draw, and the measurable ways you will impact the world. Remember that developing a vision statement is an ongoing process. As you seek the Lord, He will continually redefine it for you, and make it clearer to you.

A vision that is God-breathed is often overwhelming and in most cases may not be achievable by a single generation. Moses had vision, but it was Joshua's generation that carried the Israelites through to the Promised Land. David wanted to build God a temple, but it was ultimately left to his son, Solomon, to bring the vision to pass. Elijah eventually passed his mantle on to Elisha. Don't let the enormity of what God directs you to build intimidate you. Great visions, executed in excellence, take time, serve to galvanize people, change the world, and bring glory to the Lord.

Core Values

Core values are the heart of any strong vision and ministry. These are shared, whether spoken or not. They are not without foundation; they are already reflected in all that you do. Values are the point of commonality among members and serve to determine what will potentially attract others. Core values are essentially *the things that are important to you.* In our ministry, prayer, cultural diversity, excellence and innovation, creativity, and change are among our shared values. During new members' orientation, every candidate is provided with this information. This helps them to decide whether or not they are comfortable enough to join us. It is frustrating to invest time in someone, only to have them leave because their expectations we not met. Between five and fifteen is a good number of stated core values.

A Creed

A *creed* or *statement of beliefs* is an instrument that we should be familiar with. It is a statement of our essential doctrine. Your creed is what you believe the Scriptures teach about God, His church, our relationship to Him, one another, and the world.

Developing these items should not be done in haste. They will take time, dialogue, and careful consideration of every aspect of your ministry and its vision. All of these are essential elements needed in moving toward creating your own culture.

Once these four things have been assembled, it will be essential to effectively and regularly communicate each one to your leadership and congregation in order for them to take effect. Write about them, preach about them, teach about them, and as a congregation demonstrate and regularly point to them. Utilize every available tool to communicate your ministry's mission, vision, and values such as newsletters, the Internet, printed materials, dramas and skits. Make them a part of every new member's orientation, your illustrated sermons, special events, and advertisement.

In summation, let's look at how these four are related. Your mission statement points to why your ministry exists. For example: "to serve people and touch our community". The vision determines the specific things—mostly long-term—that your ministry engages in and puts legs on your mission. For example, you have a vision to build a 10,000 square-foot. youth center to reach area youth. Core values will state what is important to your ministry and those who join it. In this case you may discover that restoring broken homes is important. The connection might be that by reaching the children through your future youth center,

CREATING CULTURE TAKES FAITH, TIME, WORK, AND REQUIRES CONSTANT, DELIBERATE, AND STRATEGIC ACTION.

you create a sense of family for them. Finally, your creed provides the theological overview of what you believe the Bible says about God, His church, His people, and the interrelated relationships between them all.

A good example of combining culture, vision, and shared values is the nation of Israel. Israel was a planned community with a deliberately planned culture. With specific detail, God gave direction for a community that would eventually birth eternal life. Creating culture takes faith, time, work, and requires constant, deliberate, and strategic action. Intended actions produce success.

"The plans of the diligent lead surely to plenty, But those of everyone who is hasty, surely to poverty" (Proverbs 21:5).

CHAPTER 7

EXCELLENCE

"It pleased Darius to set over the kingdom one hundred and twenty satraps, to be over the whole kingdom; and over these, three governors, of whom Daniel was one, that the satraps might give account to them, so that the king would suffer no loss. Then this Daniel distinguished himself above the governors and satraps, because an excellent spirit was in him; and the king gave thought to setting him over the whole realm" (Daniel 6:1-3).

Daniel provides a perfect example of what *excellence* will produce in our lives and in our ministries, if we embrace it. Notice the Bible says he had an *excellent spirit*. Certainly you've met people who possess an excellent spirit. It's sheer joy to watch them work. You've seen it in the waiter who had perfect timing, knew his menu well, and served you as though nobody else in the restaurant existed. His excellence compelled you to increase his tip. If you returned to that particular restaurant and asked for the waiter by name, you would be excited at the prospect of receiving excellent service again.

There may be an outstanding musician who performs

effortlessly, while causing goose bumps to dance down your spine. Excellence is noticeable and unforgettable.

Last year, I purchased a new car. I had test-driven a few of the German exports, but after a couple bad experiences I decided to try Lexus. When I arrived to pick up my car,

**EXCELLENCE IS NOTICEABLE AND
UNFORGETTABLE.**

I was amazed to find a gentlemen waiting whose job was to help customers understand the features of their new car. He went over every detail for nearly an hour, and even set the radio to my favorite stations. I was so impressed! I knew I would return to the dealership in the future, because of the excellent service I had received. In the past, this transaction took about fifteen minutes as I was shown a few basic features, handed the owner's manual, and sent on my way. Excellence is not a matter of happenstance: It is very deliberate.

Those who *pretend* to have an excellent spirit do not readily fool others; their motives are easily discerned. In the book of Daniel, King Darius—who had to be very

**EXCELLENCE IS NOT A MATTER
OF HAPPENSTANCE: IT IS VERY
DELIBERATE.**

discerning in his position—could clearly see that Daniel's interest was to serve him, and give him his very best. He

knew Daniel's *operating in excellence* was not just a means to
an end. Excellence was a part of him. In fact, verse three
states that he had an excellent spirit. When one has a spirit
of excellence they can only do things one way, the right
way.

There is a particular dimension to excellence that
makes it so appealing—selflessness. Selfless giving is not
just a performance held to manipulate those being served.
It flows out of a desire to see things done well. There is
satisfaction that comes in knowing that things are done in
the best possible manner. Philippians 2:3-11 states:

> "Let nothing be done through selfish ambition or conceit, but
> in lowliness of mind let each esteem others better than himself.
> Let each of you look out not only for his own interests, but also
> for the interests of others. Let this mind be in you which was also
> in Christ Jesus, who, being in the form of God, did not consider it
> robbery to be equal with God, but made Himself of no reputation,
> taking the form of a bondservant, and coming in the likeness
> of men. And being found in appearance as a man, He humbled
> Himself and became obedient to the point of death, even the
> death of the cross. Therefore God also has highly exalted Him and
> given Him the name which is above every name, that at the name
> of Jesus every knee should bow, of those in heaven, and of those
> on earth, and of those under the earth, and that every tongue
> should confess that Jesus Christ is Lord, to the glory of God the
> Father."

Daniel moved in a spirit of excellence and benefited
greatly as a result. While it may not be the primary motive,
when you move in excellence, there is always positive
return. Daniel didn't perform his duties with an eye on

the king's reward. His desire was always to please the Lord first and therefore he did everything as unto the Lord. In Ephesians 6:7, the apostle Paul exhorts us to do the same. There is such liberty that comes with expecting nothing from man and everything from God, including the favor of man. I believe Daniel had this revelation.

King Darius preferred Daniel because of Daniel's excellent spirit and corresponding actions resulting from his disposition. He gained stature in both God's and Darius's kingdoms and became an influential leader. When we have influence, people listen; our voices are heard and our opinions matter.

People of Influence Get Things Done

When your voice echoes the sentiments of God's heart, even nations can be changed. May those to whom God has granted this sort of influence and favor recognize the significance of their words and actions, and humbly avail themselves to God in furtherance of His kingdom.

DANIEL'S EXCELLENT SPIRIT ALLOWED HIM TO BE STRATEGICALLY POSITIONED BY GOD TO IMPACT THE WORLD AND ELEVATE THE NAME OF THE LORD.

King Darius was more than happy to make Daniel governor over his kingdom, and to set him over the other governors and leaders. He recognized the spirit of excellence in this promising young man. Daniel had consistently proven himself, distinguishing himself above his fellow Israelites and other leaders as well. He was promoted and entrusted to serve in a place of great authority and significance. Excellence sets you apart. You become the standard. Daniel's excellent spirit allowed him to be strategically positioned by God to impact the world and elevate the name of the Lord.

A Church in Transition

"Sing to the LORD, For He has done excellent things; This is known in all the earth" (Isaiah 12:5).

Many of us who were brought up in the church learned to accept mediocrity in our lives. The thought that "simple and lowly was more Godly" played a significant part of our belief system. We were conditioned to overlook the obvious. Now, I don't want to put down the efforts and struggles of those who have gone before us. Very often, the lack of excellence in their time was directly tied to a lack of resources or know-how. They worked with what they had in both resources and perspective. What we've learned today is that mediocrity doesn't work. The members of our churches work, live, and play everyday in a world where excellence is both pursued and rewarded. We can't afford to have people come into our churches and feel as though they've stepped back in time. This won't draw them in, or compel them into the kingdom. Unfortunately, this has been more the rule than the exception. Thank God for the progression and forward thinking that is now infiltrating the church.

How we act and what we do in our churches have to be founded upon the Word of God. Excellence, I am pleased to say, is very much a God thing. Isaiah says that God does everything in excellence and everyone knows it (see Isaiah 12:5). The word on the street in Isaiah's day was that our God was a first-class God. A trend-setter! He is still a God of excellence and, I believe, He expects us to be excellent in every way as well.

The truth is that we've always expected excellence from the secular world, while mediocrity has been widely accepted as the modus operandi of the church. However,

WE'VE ALWAYS EXPECTED EXCELLENCE FROM THE SECULAR WORLD, WHILE MEDIOCRITY HAS BEEN WIDELY ACCEPTED AS THE MODUS OPERANDI OF THE CHURCH.

in the past couple decades, the church has seriously considered its presentation to the world. We've begun to ask the serious questions and make critical changes to the way we exhibit ourselves. For many contemporary leaders and church members, this newly established philosophy is a long awaited, yet welcome change.

With this new transition towards excellence, thoughts about the irrelevance of the church in today's society are eroding. A much wider net is being cast and all the earth is being compelled to give the church a second look. This is because the church is beginning to act like its head, Jesus Christ.

Excellence

We are stepping it up in our churches, becoming a strong contender in the market place in the areas of television production, multi-media, printed material, programming, and the use of technology. I'm using the business term "marketplace" because, whether or not we want to admit it, we are in a fierce battle with world systems for the attention of people. In addition to prayer and other spiritual disciplines, it also takes strategic and creative methods to reach the world. Intelligence and strategic planning are not sins. They work hand-in-hand with faith and obedience to God. They also play a big part in becoming a church with a spirit of excellence upon it.

> EXCELLENCE SHOULD BE THE NORM,
> NOT THE EXCEPTION.

Why Excellence?

"O LORD, our Lord, How excellent is Your name in all the earth!" (Psalm 8:9).

Excellence must be in all we do for a number of reasons. First, it is a part of God's very nature. In fact, according to the psalmist, His name is excellent in all the earth. As we serve as representatives of God's kingdom, excellence should be the norm, not the exception.

EXCELLENCE IS AN EXPRESSION OF GOD,
IT ATTRACTS PEOPLE, WHILE MEDIOCRITY
IN THE CHURCH REPELS THEM.

Here's another reason: The world understands excellence. I often think about our Christian rhetoric and how it contradicts so many of our actions. Worldly people are not blind; they can clearly see our hypocrisy, and they are neither moved nor convinced by our words and actions. It's true that non-believers may not be able to comprehend spiritual things, but they can certainly understand the things that the spirit produces. Because excellence is an expression of God, it attracts people, while mediocrity in the church repels them.

A third reason for excellence is opportunity. If we are going to reach the world with the gospel, we need opportunities to do so. Excellence provides a platform for extended dialog with the world. Mel Gibson's movie, *Passion of the Christ*, put the church in a position to talk about redemption and the price that Jesus paid for it. Never before in modern times has the church held the attention of such a broad audience.

I recently visited Dr. Robert Schuller's Crystal Cathedral in Garden Grove, California. The Crystal Cathedral has been the subject of many news features because of its phenomenal architectural design. It is a testament to God's creative ability as expressed through one of His servants. It's also a place of excellence. As I walked the grounds, I was proud to be called a Christian. While there, Dr. Schuller shared in a repetitive phrase what he feels is the present responsibility of the church. He said, "we are to turn skeptics into seekers, seekers into believers and believers into achievers."

Excellence

People who have never been interested in the church before are now interested in the ways of the King and His kingdom. Whenever there are powerful demonstrations of excellence by the church, the world is attracted.

It's important to note that excellence brings glory to our God. We should always work to produce excellence in all that we do and encourage every member of our church and family to do the same.

Excellence & Excellent People

We work diligently to encourage excellence in our team at Harvest. We may not always get it right the first time, but we continue to strive for excellence. I believe it begins with understanding of the importance of excellence and actively desiring it in all that we do. For instance, I am always concerned about the women who come to Harvest when it's raining or snowing, and in particular those with babies in strollers. I mentioned this once during a service. I was elated when I pulled up one Sunday morning and saw young men holding umbrellas lined up, awaiting the arriving cars, and escorting women into the building. Someone on the team had addressed my concern with excellence.

There is an intrinsic desire within people of excellence to constantly take things to a higher level. It's something they pursue and they never need an audience to do so because it is a personal choice. Excellence is the refusal to settle for the status quo; it is a matter of going beyond the call of duty, striving to exceed expectations, rather than just meet them.

Make Excellence a Part of Your Ministry's Culture?

Some people may think that excellence is over the top. They may see the price that it costs to be a person of excellence or be deterred by the required sacrifices. They may even launch a subtle campaign to undermine you. You must defend and uphold excellence at all times and at all levels. If you lose a few people in the process, pray for their growth and move on. They may fight against you today, but as they proceed down life's road, the mere encounter with another excellent spirit will stir something within their heart. Given time, they will see the fruit that grows from operating in excellence. Never apologize for operating in excellence.

The first step towards excellence is to *think in excellence*. Hide it in your heart. Now that you see excellence from a biblical perspective, embrace the significance of it. As you evaluate your ministry, look around and ask yourself, "Is this

JUST BECAUSE SOMETHING IS NOT BROKE, DOES NOT MEAN THAT YOU DO NOT NEED TO FIX OR ENHANCE IT.

excellent? Can it be done better?" Just because something is not broke, does not mean that you do not need to fix or enhance it. Always look to improve upon, upgrade, and do things in a new and better way—the way of excellence. Challenge yourself to process everything through this new paradigm.

Excellence

Sometimes excellence involves doing simple things. For example, we have asked our entire leadership team to pick up any piece of paper they see on the floor of our church. It does not matter whose job it is to clean; it matters who the church belongs to—our Lord Jesus. Our God is a God of excellence and we will work to be like Him, taking ownership as divine partners with the Lord.

Promote and celebrate excellence. When you see excellence among those you serve, acknowledge it and encourage them. People love to be honored and recognized. It produces in them the desire to operate in excellence at all times.

Communicate excellence in every possible way. Speak on it, preach about it, print it, sing about it and point to it as often as you see it or even think about it.

Do it! Put excellence into practice in everything you do. It may not be "the most excellent way" every time, but you should always strive towards it. This should be the case on a personal level, as well as throughout your organization. It may cost a little more in the beginning, but the harvest will be commensurate with the seeds planted.

Always remember, excellence is a God thing!

FOOTNOTES

[1]Biblical Healing
Publisher: Osborn International
© 2001 T. L. Osborn
ISBN: 9780879431433

[2]Tommy Barnett
Hidden Power
Charisma House
© 2002 Tommy Barnett
ISBN: 0-88419-771-9

[3]George Barna
The Power of Vision
Regal Books
© 1992, 2003, George Barna
ISBN 0-8307-3255-1

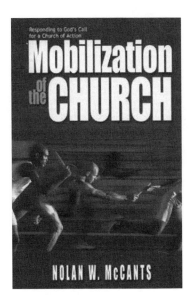

Here is another powerful title that is available by Nolan W. McCants

Mobilization of the Church
Responding to God's call for a Church of Action

Workshops, Training and Consulting

Nolan McCants is available to serve your ministry. Call today to schedule him for your next leadership training session, conference, or retreat. He brings a wealth of experience from both business and ministry that will help to enhance your ministry. He is also available for consulting assignments to aid senior leaders in evaluating and perfecting ministry administration and operations.

Contact us at:
McCants Ministries
P. O. Box 472
Naperville, IL 60567
630-904-6262

www.nolanmccants.com